Faith
Courage
Wisdom
Strength
And Hope

Inspirational Poetry
That Comes from the Heart

Stacey Chillemi

PublishAmerica
Baltimore

First printing

At the specific preference of the author, PublishAmerica allowed this work to remain exactly as the author intended, verbatim, without editorial input.

ISBN: 1-4137-7588-8
PUBLISHED BY PUBLISHAMERICA, LLLP
www.publishamerica.com
Baltimore

Printed in the United States of America

Dedicated to my husband Michael,

my three children Michael, Alexis and Anthony

Foreword

We must view life as each day is the first day of the rest of our lives. We should keep an outlook in our minds about life, as each day is the opportunity for a new start. We must learn to live each day to the fullest, and we can do that only if we learn to accept that we cannot change the past. We cannot stop a tragedy from entering our lives. If you were struck by an illness, disorder, disability or disease, you cannot tell it to go away. We have to accept what has happened, accept the new person we have become by the tragedy that has entered our life and love ourselves no matter what. No one is perfect. We all have flaws. The present is now and we hold the key to the future. It is time to create the new you.

Happiness and success comes with persistence and hard work. We must have a goal and work hard. Follow your hearts to true happiness. You must have a destination, a goal and a plan. You are special. You can be anything you want too. Your family loves you, your friends, spouse and the world loves you. Now it is your turn to love yourself. These poems in this book will give you the faith, hope, courage, strength to be happy, and love life. If you cannot find happiness in the present, you will never find it in the future. Those who find true happiness pursue the goal of achieving as much success, and finding as much happiness, as possible every day of their lives.

Many people think that happiness lies in how much material wealth you accumulated. Nevertheless, we must find happiness within ourselves—not in the external world.

Happiness comes from within and from making others happy. Each day we have a new opportunity to find happiness; and unless we are able to learn to be happy on a day-to-day basis, we will probably never find true happiness. There are situations, such as getting an illness, disorder, disease, disability or some type of sickness, when we find ourselves trapped, full of anger not knowing where to turn or what to do. The anger of losing control of our lives. You may feel like life is meaningless and happiness is no longer an option.

My poems will show you otherwise. I will show you through my poetry that there is no reason to be anger. Love yourself as your love ones love you. Life is meaningless unless you can love, be happy and bring your happiness to others. As you read my poetry, you will see a completely new meaning of live. In addition, Faith will once again be apart of your life.

Introduction

"Faith, Courage, Wisdom, Strength and Hope," is a collection of poems that
Inspire your mind, body and soul. This book will give you the inspiration to want to live life
To the fullest and be the best you can be. The poems in this book have been written to inspire and comfort readers, as well as to give you a completely different view of life.

The poems make you realize that you are special and you have the potential to love yourself and love life. Each of us has a responsibility to try to make us feel good about ourselves. We need to love ourselves, be proud of ourselves, accept ourselves and make ourselves happy. One of the best ways to find happiness for ourselves is to seek to bring happiness to others.

We all have our share of troubles in life; some suffer from illness, disorders, diseases and other obstacles that come our way. We need to keep our spirits high on a consistent basis. This is easier said than done for most of us. However, there are things we can do to help us bring happiness into our lives. Positive thinking has long been recognized as a valuable tool for coping with life. However, sometimes it is hard, if not impossible, to think positively. What can we do to make our journey for a positive outlook on life easier?

Words of wisdom can be a very powerful tool to help the mental healing process. In order to succeed in life and get through the loop poles that are sometimes thrown at us we must learn the magic of accepting and loving ourselves. There is a certain kind of magical feeling that occurs inside us when we learn to accept who we are and love ourselves for who we are.

There are times when we faced with illnesses, disorders, disabilities some type of tragedy that causes us to lose contact with ourselves and the world in which we live. Our happiness begins to fade and our heart begins to grow heavy. This affects the way we think, live, feel and the way we look at life.

None of us can be happy all the time. During times of tragedy, it is natural and even beneficial to be sad, but not to hold unhappy, anger or any negative emotion that takes control. We must heal ourselves emotionally and spiritually.

Contents

A New Beginning

There comes a time when the meaning of life begins to make sense,
At first we may not understand why things happen the way they do,
The sky at first may look dark,
The path one needs to walk down may be hard to see,
Remember the stars are the brightest when the nights seem the darkest
Look up at the stars and make a wish
One wish
Never let a disorder control one's destiny,
Move forward,
Never move backwards
Plan a positive, fulfilling future,
Never let your tragedy control your mind, body and soul,
Never give up,
Be in control,
Accept yourself,
Accept your disorder,
Love yourself now and forever,
Developing a disorder
Makes you feel barricaded against a corner
Giving up is not an option,
The present is now,
Today is a new day,
If you stay down life will pass you by,
Therefore, each time you fall
Help yourself get up,
Fight the battle
Win your battle,
To win the battle all you need to do is try,
Winning the battle is teaching yourself how to live a healthy productive
life,
Helping yourself cope,

A New Beginning, continued

Life may not always be what you planned it to be,
The road you lead may have some u-turns involved,
Do not fear,
For change can be good,
Follow the path that was destined for you,
The sun is now shinning,
You can now see your path
There is a plan, a destiny that awaits you,
Do not question your destiny,
Do not ask questions such as "why me?"
Follow life's journey the one that has been planned for you.
Do not be afraid,
Take one day at a time,
Be proud of who you are,
Walk with courage and your head up high,
Believe in yourself,
Focus on the positive,
For the footsteps imbedded in ground of your new path will become the
solid foundation to you future.

Love and Friendship

Optimistic people bring a sense of hope into world
Encouraging people bring a new meaning to life.
They help you see past the clouds on a glooming day
They bring sunlight everyday
Each day has so much more meaning when their spent with people who
believe.
Happiness is when you are with people who love you for who you are not
what you should be,
This is the true meaning of love and friendship,
Each day you are reborn with love and joy when you realize that you have
people by your side that care.
It is wonderful to know that people care for each other.
Our life becomes one happy dream.
People teach you the true meaning of love through their actions
It is important to give back others
Having a heart filled with gold is useless when you have no one to share.

Special Gifts

Everyone has special gifts
Everyone is talented
Everyone can achieve his or her dreams
The future is still to come
The present is now
The past is behind us.
Your mind, body and soul hold special gifts and talents,
Your mind is the workshop where you cultivate all your thoughts, dreams
and wishes.
Your spirit is where you hold all your strength and courage
Your soul is the spiritual body where your emotions live inside you
And your heart is the key that locks them all together as one
You have inner strength,
Courage,
Wisdom,
Faith,
Hope
Use your gifts to your advantage
Do not let them sit and rot away.

The Power of Ambition

Every morning when I wake up,
I awake looking forward to what I can accomplish.
Developing positive goals,
Realizing the power of ambition
The power of change,
Life consists of positive transformation.
Nothing is final unless you let it be
Open you eyes to a broad pathway
A journey that will lead you to a fulfilling future.
You choose the path you take
You prepare the draft of your life
You have control
You have the ability to plan your destiny,
Not everything is your life is planned
Everyday is a new day
You are capable and worthy of becoming who you want to be
Never give up
Have determination
Follow your heart and all your dreams will come true.

Believe In Your Heart

I woke up one night in the hours of darkness,
I sat up straight in my bed to find a shimmering light in my closet,
But their where no lights on in the room,
I got up and went slowly toward the closet,
To find a pair of gold wings,
An angel was standing by my side,
"What do I do with these gold wings?" I asked the angel
"Put the wings on my child." Answered the angel
I put the wings on flew to a place that had many stars,
The angel then appeared and said, "Follow your heart, your goals and
your dreams."
Only you know what is right for you
Anything is possible
Miracles do come true,
Hope and dreams are a reality if let them be,
Life can be wonderful if you let it be,
The world is at your feet
Therefore, there is no time waste,
Start flying to the stars,
The bright star in the sky created especially for you,
Therefore, there is no time to lose go find your bright star,
When you find it, open the magic door
Out will come gifts,
Waiting for you to explore,
So believe in your dreams
Follow your heart
Your world can be a happier place as long as you believe.

Love and Care for Yourself

Your face will not glow with happiness unless you love yourself,
The birds will not sing songs unless you sing with them,
The flowers will not blossom unless you water them,
The beautiful smell they carry will not breeze through the universe we take
care of them,
Everything is meaningless unless you love and take care of yourself…
Love yourself,
Accept yourself,
Believe in yourself,
Believe in your wishes,
Believe in your dreams,
Hopes and desires.

Loving You for Who You Are

Your kisses and hugs are so sweet,
Your smiles bring me joy,
Be proud of yourself and everything you have done.
Your love lies in your heart,
Everyone's heart that you have touched,
Your love is special,
No one can take your love from me
Every person you have touched,
No one can change the way I feel for you,
Alternatively, the way others feel for you.
My life is devoted to you.
You are so special,
So blessed,
Having your love in my life,
I feel I am capable to share every feeling,
Every thought,
Every aspect of my life with you-

Loving Yourself

Life should feel as you would feel waking up on a sunny day,
Feeling the warmth of the sun as the sunlight peers through the window
shades.
It is a refreshing feeling,
A feeling of joy,
A peaceful feeling
The planet is blessed to have you in our world,
As a person, you are as beautiful as the pedals of a rose
The laughter of children's voices,
When I look outside my bedroom window,
I see the beauty of the world that God has created and the window of
opportunities it holds.
I need to feel good about myself,
I need to have hope
I must succeed,
I must love myself
Accept who I am
I must be an inspiration to others,
As others were for me.

Philosophy of Survival

The past is no longer here,
Your disability is now a part of you,
The present is today,
Survival of the fittest,
This means accepting your disorder,
Loving who you are,
Making each day a positive one,
Never feeling sorry for yourself,
The future is waiting,
So start planning now,
Begin by challenging yourself,
Focusing on not what your disorder is doing to you,
Nevertheless, what can you do with your disorder to help yourself and to
help other people.

The Past Is Behind Us the Present Is Now

The past no longer exists,
Our future relies on the present
The future is still to come
The present is now
Take your inner energy and focus it on now
Enthusiasm is the tool for a happy future,
Get up in the morning and be happy that you are here
Look out your window and notice the bright sun
The essence of the flowers
The smell of fresh cut grass
Use your enthusiasm to accomplish all your goals
Your dreams,
Wishes,
The will to succeed is the answer to true happiness.

Succeed in Life

Life comes with obstacles,
Obstacles that must be pursued,
No matter how rough the obstacle,
You will succeed by trying your best,
Failure does not exist if you try,
Taking "one day at a time,
You cannot change the past,
The best is yet to come,
The present is now,
Focus and work on the present,
Success will follow in the future,
Focus on the goals that you create for yourself,
Change is wonderful,
Do not fear change,
Chang is wonderful,
Today is the beginning to a new destiny,
The mind is a powerful tool that has the strength to achieve,
Create a plan to help cope with your discomfort
Believe in yourself and focus on the positive aspects of life,
Take "one step at a time",
Focus on what you have, not what you do not have,
Life is what you make it,
So look at the positive and over power the negative,
You control your life,
Never let life control you…

The Blessing of Today

You must feel in your heart and soul that you are special,
Reward yourself each day for all the wonderful things you have accom-
plished,
Close your eyes and thank God for today,
Because today was a gift given to you,
Not everyone has the gift of today,
So use it meaningfully,
Find time to smell the flowers,
Share your inner beauty,
Share your smiles,
Each day is a new day,
So use it wisely,
Positively,
Not negatively
Your world will blossom if you believe in yourself
Believe
Believe and your dreams will become a reality
A life full of joy and happiness

The Journey

Waking up each morning to venture a new challenge,
The beauty of life waits,
Search your soul and listen to what your heart desires,
The heart is a strong instrument,
It keeps you alive not only physically, but also emotionally,
If you listen closely to your heart,
You will feel the messages it sends to you,
Enjoy the beauty of life,
Epilepsy will not stop you from the joys of life,
You are in charge of your destiny,
You are in charge of your inner strength,
Use your dreams to lead you to a new destiny,
Helping yourself and helping others,
Everyone has a purpose and a direction in life,
What is your purpose in life?
Each moment awaits you,
So begin your journey now,
Believe in yourself and others will believe in you.

The Pathway of Hope

The mind, body and soul is a unique creation from the heavens above,
Inside us lies a person filled with hope and dreams,
A person filled with strength to achieve,
Special gifts and talents,
Follow your dreams, your desires,
You are an extraordinary person with many hopes and dreams,
Your dreams can become your reality,
If you let them,
Listen to heart not the world around you for no one knows you better than
no one knows yourself.

This Is Your Life

Disorders creates obstacles,
Inner emotions feeling as though it is difficult to focus on the things that
mean the most to you in life,
What is important is happiness,
To be happy one must follow inner dreams, passions and desires,
Suffering from epilepsy or any disorder can confuse and overwhelm one
with emotion,
Emotions you may not understand,
Do not let these emotions stop you from loving life and loving yourself,
Life is a gift from the heavens above,
Feel of anger may linger inside,
But the truth is "This is your Life',
You are not a product from a store that you can exchange for a new one,
There is a reason you were blessed on this earth,
Search your soul,
Seek the truth,
In addition, you will find your destiny,
Why you were chosen to live this life,
Have faith, hope and believe in yourself,
You destiny lies in front of you,
Open your eyes and your mind to the pathway of your destination.

May Your Days All Be Blessed

May all your days
All be blessed
With the existence
Of someone who cares for you
Accepts you and your flaws
Will watch over you
Protect you
Care for you
Throughout eternity

Being By Your Side

May you always have someone who loves you for who you,
The true spiritual being that lives inside you,
Who will stand by your side through better or for worse,
In sickness and in health,
Prompting you to believe,
To believe in life,
To believe in yourself,
Giving you the encouragement to believe that wishes and dreams can
come true,
If you believe
Giving you the strength and guidance that you need
May you always have someone to love,
And someone to love you back,
May you always have that special someone,
Who loves you for who you are
Someone to take care of you when you are sick
To hold you when you are cold,
To make you laugh when you are sad,
Encouraging you to follow your hopes and dreams,
Giving you the energy to succeed,
Holding you hand when you need the touch of a hand
The hand from that special someone
Who will love you through eternity
Who will help you during your hard times
Glorify you during the good times
Each day is a new beginning
With new things to encounter
May you have that special someone to accompany you during you new
beings
To be bonded by your side
To help you each moment of the day
To hug you with tight hugs and soft kisses.

Our World is Full of Good People

People who care always come to help us in our time of need
They show care in their eyes
The love follows through their actions
Never discredit the people on this planet
Because many have hearts of gold
They are willing to bring you a rainbow
After every storm

Special Someone

There is always someone on this planet willing to love you for who you are
Who wants to love
Take care of you
Give themselves and everything they have to you
Protect you
Never judge you
Every person has a special someone that they are destined to meet
Keep your eyes open
Because they are on their way
If you have not met them already
So open your heart
Let the love pour in
Because that special someone is on their way.

Have Faith

No matter where in the world you live
There is always that special someone waiting for you
To accept you for you are
How you look,
How you feel,
How you act,
Have faith in people
Have faith in the world
There is no reason to give up on life
Life has not given up on you.

The Blessing of Communication

We are blessed with the words of wisdom
We all have gifts to share
Stories to tell
Let us all learn from each other
To exchange words of wisdom
To share the positive things that we learned from our past
Therefore, others will not fall into the traps laid on the paths below us
The ability to communicate is a wonderful gift
One does not have to communicate through their mouth
But through their actions
We are all touched in a positive way through the ability to communicate
Spiritually, verbally or through the actions of one's ability to communicate

Youthfulness

The sun brings brightness
To help share a beautiful day
With the people who matter the most
As long as our hearts stay young
Our happiness will prolong
Giving meaning to life
And laughter and happiness to the children who will hold the key to the
next generation
Let the love and truthfulness that you hold free
Share it with the ones that mean the most to us
The children who roam our earth and are responsible for our youthfulness
Out body yearns for love
No life is complete without love
Love cannot be given to someone unless you love yourself
So look in your mirror
Be proud of who you are

A Word of Wisdom

We are God's servants placed on earth
Act on earth
As you would in the great heavens above

When in Fear Help is Near

If you are fearful
Lonely
Or in question
Reach out to someone you trust
Someone to fill your heart with faith
Courage and direction
Someone to fill your heart with hope

Empty Your Heavy Heart

If you are fearful
Lonely
Or in question
Reach out to someone you trust
Someone to fill your heart with faith
Courage and direction
Someone to fill your heart with hope

The Wonders of the World

As I get older
I begin to think more
Who I am
What have I accomplished?
Where am I going in life?
What should I do?
Be thankful for what you have
Be proud of yourself
Love yourself
Accept yourself
Plan goals
The wonder of the world lies in front of us
Listen to your heart
Follow your dreams

Destiny

We may not always understand why we were put on this earth
Nevertheless, there is a reason and answer for everything
As time flutters on
You will understand your reason
And your destiny on earth

A Time to Rejoice

You must look at each day not as just another day
But as a special day
A day to conquer your obstacles
And to win your battles
Celebrate the feeling of accomplishment
Rejoice what you have in your life.

Be Thankful

Be thankful for what you have
Many others are not as blessed as you are
And not materialistically
Be thankful for the people in your life
Be thankful that you have a life
Be thankful that there is people in your life that love you
Want to be with you
Want to help you
Care for you
Be thankful that you people in your life that inspire you
Moreover, give you inspiration
Hope,
Joy
People who help lift the burdens from us
In addition, replace them with hope
Be thankful for the air you breathe
The flowers you smile
The peaceful of the ocean waves
Be thankful for you.

Give to Others

If you love others
Others will love you
If you care for others
Others will care for you
If you help others
Others will help you
Give to others
As they give an to you

Follow the Pathway

No one knows where are paths will lead us
We need to journey down the path and follow where our heart leads us
The trail may be long
Never give up
The one's who follow the trail to the end receive true happiness
The one is who give
End up lost and unhappy

True Happiness

When you know people you care for are there for you
True happiness will always be in your heart
Displayed through your actions

Hope

Hope is walking through sands
Listening to the ocean shore
Looking up into the sky
Seeing the moon ever so bright
Everywhere you look is a bright glow
From the hundreds of stars that shine that night
Suddenly a shouting star flies by
You close your eyes and make a wish
The feeling of hopes fills your soul
For a moment, you feel a moment of peace
Because you believe
Believe in wishes
Dreams
Anything that brings you happiness

Another Way

When an obstacle occurs
It causes to block your path
Do not stop your journey
Take another path
A path with fewer difficulties to walk
There is always another way
Do not fear change
Change is good
We all have barriers
Obstacles
Problems and pain
We cannot plan our lives
However, we can make sure we stay on track

Looking Inside

Life is a giving place
It is a generous place
Sometimes we get too much
And instead of appreciating our gifts
We reject them
Because we judge the gift from the outside box
Instead of looking on what is inside the box

True Love is Awaiting to be Found

Somewhere there is your true love
Just waiting to recognized
Someone that will love you
No matter what

Living Life Positively

Living life positively will make you feel alive
You will fill the love in your hear
The wisdom in your mind
And the happiness in your soul

Making Dreams into a Reality

When your heart is full with happiness
You feel the energy to follow your dreams and make them into a reality
You have what it takes
To help you reach your destiny
Your qualities are gifts that given to you by the heavens above
Take those talents an use them
Not just on yourself, but on others also
These will lead you to a life full of happiness.
As you, practice your beliefs
And the gifts that were given to you
You will feel a sense of strength and courage that will begin to grow inside
of you.
The world is full with opportunities
Just waiting for you to explore
Believe in yourself
That is all it takes
Once you believe in yourself
Courage,
Hope,
Faith
Strength will develop inside you
Making all your dreams a reality.

Do Not Be Ashamed of Who You Are

Do not ashamed of who you are
You are special
Your heart is full with love
Let your kindness
And your caring ness be known to the world
Be the person you always want to be
Live in joy and happiness
Nothing can hold you back
Unless, you let it
You cannot move forward in life unless you take chances
Find your strengths and build on them each day
Share them with others
Learn from the people around you
Always be proud of who you are
You are a special person with so much to give
So many people will learn from you if you let them
You will learn from them
You can open people's eyes
Lead them to new journeys to follow
Including your own journey, this is just about to begin.

The Magic of Believing in Yourself

If you have one set goal
And you belief in yourself
If you have faith and hope
You will succeed in what ever you put your mind too.

What to Do When We Have a Disability

Most people with a disability, illness or disorder look at themselves as
different
Some have anger built up inside
Some pity themselves, "oh why me, why me?"
What people do not know is that we can use our disability to better
ourselves
Help the people around us
There is no need to feel that life has ended because a barrier has entered
our lives
You are special and you can use your disability to help other see that life
has not ended
Our life has just begun
A new path was entered our journey
Have courage and take that new path
Change is good
Change leads to new and better things
Remember
No one is flawless
We all have our flaws
Yes, I have a disability and nothing is going to change
How can I use this disability to empower myself and help other see a new
light?

What to Do When We Have a Disability, continued

If you have a pair of wings in your room
Do not just stare at them
Put them on and soar through the skies
While you were fling through the clouds and seeing life in a completely
new light
Use what you learned to help yourself and help yourself by helping others
The wise look answers for inner healing
They create goals
Go after them with great ambition
Be proud who you are
Go after your dream
One accomplishment is years of satisfaction
Love yourself
There is nothing to be ashamed of
Go after your dreams
Accomplish your goals
Life is a learning process
We learn from life and we teach others what we have learned

There is a Plan for Us

Every one has a predestined path
The heavens have a plan for us on earth
While on earth, we will have to make sacrifices
Some may not be so easy
However, with strength and determination we can conquer all
Our path contains obstacles
Sometimes we may trip and fall
Nevertheless, if you fall just do not lay there
Get up and continue your journey
Have faith and hope
The answers to your questions always lie in your heart
Believe my friend
Have courage in yourself
Have courage in the world in which you live
When you feel tired
Do not give up
Keeping going till you get to your destination
Sometimes we may not understand why things happen the way they do
However, there is a reason for everything
Life may seem unfair sometimes
Focus on the good
There is always a pot of gold at the end of the trail
Getting there is the challenge
Do not give up
Do not doubt your abilities
You can do anything
Be anything
Accomplish anything you put your mind too.

Today, I See

Written by Stephanie S. Sawyer

Today, I see.
I see past the brown speckled leaves
which adorn the bare bush
straggling for life.

Today, I see.
I see far beyond the faint thinness and sprawl
which covers the bush.

Today, I see.
I see a new spark
a root of new sprout reaching up to the sun.
It struggles.
It hopes.
It demands.
It bursts forth!

Lo, I see.
New life,
the same root.
A fresh bud.

Today, I see, continued

Today, I see.
I see health from the root stem.

The same bush is before me.
To which shall I look?

Today, I see
life from the root stem,
Love bursting forth as growth bedecks growth.

Hope cannot fail.

Today, I see.
I see healthier tone
as it merges with hope.
Wisdom springs forth as the sage of the past,
casting aside all the dark from the pain.

Today, I see,
and give thanks.

About The Writer:

Stephanie S. Sawyer is the author if FACING ME (Publish America), an inspirational autobiography focused on hope, and featuring corrective brain surgery. The Epilepsy Foundation has recognized her dedication to outreach and education on seizures.

Ms. Sawyer is a classical pianist and private piano teacher. She is dedicated to sharing the joy of music as inspiration for her students. She has also directed various church choirs.

Coping with your Life

People who are able to cope
With their disorder, disability, illness or any tragedy, that enters their lives
Are the people who have confidence in themselves
The people who take the time out of their busy lives to set productive goals
They do not procrastinate
So do not lie to themselves or to others
They try their hardest
Fight for a cause
They do not think about failing
They focus on succeeding
They accept themselves and love themselves
They keep open minds
Are willing to hear what others have to say
Even though they listen to others
They still listen to their heart
Follow the directions that their inner instance tells them.
They know their strengths
They know their weaknesses
They use their strengths to their advantage
And are always working on improving their weaknesses
They have inner happiness that glows outwardly
They are not afraid to be who they are
They do not care what others think.

Empower your Life

You are the master
The chief
The one in charge
You control your destiny
You can turn any nightmare
Into a party
Take any tragedy in your life
Use your experience
As a learning experiencing
Take what you learned
Use it to help yourself
And to help other going through similar things in their life
Empower yourself
Use that power to conquer all battles
Heal yourself
Take control of your life
Plan a future full of joy and happiness
You deserve only the best
Because my friend you are special and you have the ability to be the very
best.

The Gift of Giving

Just because you are hurting does not mean you cannot help anyone else
Our greatest moments of strength come when we are hurting the most
An inner strength builds up inside
An incredible feeling of strength
A strength to overcome anything that comes your way
This special gift is given to the people who know how to use it wisely
People who will share their strength
Not just to help themselves,
But to share it with others who need help
Themselves
There are angel helpers on earth
You may be one of them
You may not even know it
So do not be selfish
Use your strength wisely
The best gift on earth is the satisfaction of helping others
And seeing their happy expressions on their face.

Happiness Cake

Writer Anonyms

1 CUP OF GOOD THOUGHTS

2 CUPS OF SACRIFICE

1 CUP OF KIND DEEDS

1 CUP OF CONSIDERATION

2 CUPS OF YOUR THOUGHTS

*Combine the ingredients and mix thoroughly. Flavor with love and kindly
service. Fold in prayers, faith and enthusiasm. Spread all into your daily
life. Blend with human kindness.*
*Serve with a constant smile and it will satisfy the hunger of many people
less fortunate than us.*
Thank the lord,
For all of his mercy,
And love,
Amen

Wish Upon a Star

I wish,
I wish,
I wish every day is a day of hope
A day filled with love
Full of faith
A day of strength to fight off any storm with one breath
A day full of kindness
And everlasting love
I wish all these things for you

In Closing, I would like to leave you with this true story.

An Angel's Helper

I was eight years old. I was worried about my mother. My mother had a hard life growing up and wanted to make up for it with her own family. I was an only child and my mother desperately wanted another child to carry the family name. She was thirty-four at the time and suffered from some medical problems, but that did not stop her from wanting her second child. Finally, her dream came true. She became pregnant at age thirty-four. She was a nervous person to begin with and having a child in her mid-thirties made her even more concerned for her child's health. My mom was beginning to think something bad might happen to the baby, so she went to get amniocentesis.

My father begged her not to get it done, but against his word, she did anyway. An amniocentesis is a common prenatal test in which a small sample of the amniotic fluid surrounding the fetus is removed and examined to see if the baby has any birth defects.

The doctor who performed the procedure did it incorrectly. The doctor withdrew the wrong amount of fluid, so instead of waiting a couple of days to withdraw the proper amount of fluid, he withdrew more the same day. In result, the baby did not have enough fluid to survive.

My mother did not think anything of it when she left the office. She did not think withdrawing double the amount of fluid would do anything to the baby. My mother did not bother to say anything that day to us.

The next morning while sleeping, I was awakened by something glowing above my bed in my bedroom. I sat straight up in bed. What was it? As I watched, the glow became larger and more radiant. I saw something in the center. Why, it was a figure of a man. The man was dressed in a robe. He looked like he was in his twenties or thirties and he had a beard. I was not scared at all.

The man moved closer to me, somehow bringing the light with him. Still shinning straight above me, he sat down on the side of my bed and said something to me. Something I did not want to hear.

"Stacey"

How do you know my name?"

He did not say.

"Listen to me," the beautiful man said.

His voice was like gold, all shimmers and lovely. He had such peace in his voice.

"Stacey, you have been very worried about your Mommy, but you don"t need to be afraid about your mother and baby"s she is carrying. It is for the best.

I was confused. I looked directly into his big brown eyes and asked, "What is for the best?"

"What I am about to tell you, may make you mad. You are not going to understand now, but later in life the pieces will unfold and you will understand why this happened."

"Understand "what?" Why what happened," I asked.

The baby your mother is carrying is dead my child!

I started yelling at him screaming, "No, No".

"The baby is in a better world, a place where he needs to be. He is in the heavens, where there is no evil and only love exists. Now you need to be there for your mother. "I am watching over your brother and I'll make sure he fine, he"ll walk the world with me. It is your job to help your mother. She needs your strength and love, because your mother's strength will diminish through this tragic event. "All right?"

Yes!" I replied. The bright figure then faded away.

My mother was leaving to go to the doctor that day. I did not say anything to her about what the angels had told me. I did not want to upset her. I felt butterflies in my stomach. I knew this would be a tragic day for all. I looked out the window as she got into the car, tears rolled down my eyes as I wept them off my face. I remember what the angel said, "You must be your mother"s strength."

That day my mother came home distraught and in tears. The doctors told she lost the baby and that she had to be hospitalized, so they could remove the baby from her body. She sat down on the couch with her face covered by her hands. I knew then that the doctor had told her. I did not ask her any questions because I did not want to upset her anymore than she already was.

The angel was right. I realized that the angel was preparing me, so I could be the angel"s helper on earth. I walked over to my mother. She looked at me and was about to tell me what I already knew. She was about to tell me, but I covered her mouth. Mother I know the angel from the heavens came and told me about your misfortune. I am sorry. I am here to give you my strength. The angel told me that you need my strength and my eternal love. I am your daughter, your pain is my pain and my strength is now yours. We will get through this together. For all things, happen for a reason. The angel said, we may not understand at first, but as times goes on we will understand. She looked stunned for a moment, a bit confused, but then she grabbed me and gave me a tight hug. We wept together and a special bond that developed between us at that moment, one that that will never diminish.

That moment was a special one. I felt such a spiritual feeling in the room when I hugged my mom. I felt the same peaceful aura in the room that I felt in my bedroom when the angel came to visit. I looked around but saw no one.

I can still hear myself offering my help to the one person in the world who meant the most to me, my mom. God had sent a messenger "the man" to prepare me for my mother"s loss and to teach me how not to be anger or blame anyone for what has happened, but to focus on the person who needed my help the most, "my mother." The man—the messenger from the heavens showed me how to move my mother through the grieving process toward healing.

The next day my father drove my mother to the hospital. She was there for two days. The first day they removed the baby that now lived in the heavens above. They kept her over night to make sure there were no complications.

When she came home, I was there to greet her. She held back the tears and it was a struggle just to smile at me. She went to room and my father followed. When he closed the door, I walked by to listen what they were saying.

"Why did I get that test done?" my mother yelled in grief. I could have had my second child. The son I always wanted. I will never get to hold him or feel his soft baby skin. I will never see him laugh. I will never see him smile.

"My sweet Tina" my father said, one day we will meet our son when we are in the heavens. The baby we would have had is resting in peace with a halo over its head. Do not blame yourself. You did what you thought was right for the welfare of the child. Death is a comma not a period. We have a future ahead of us. Who knows what God has in store? We are still young. We still can have another child. When it is our turn to fly to the heavens, we will meet our child behind the pearly gate. After that, there was a long moment of silence.

Days followed my mother was not the same mom that I knew. She was not the bubbly happy person who would greet me at the bus stop. She was grieving over the loss of the baby. Her body still thought the baby was there. She continued to fill up with breast milk and her breasts became tendered. This did not help her emotional state. She was being reminded each day of what could have been.

She moped around the house looking and feeling depressed. I remembered what the man had said, that one morning, "It is your job to help your mother. She needs your strength and love, because your mother's strength will diminish through this tragic event."

For some reason I, felt compelled to open my bible. I walked over to my desk and picked up my bible. The bible fell to the floor and opened to the book of psalm. I read the page and one of the passages caught my eye. It was Psalm 91:11. He will give his angels charge of you to guard you in all your ways.

I realized that the man, the angel that was sent to me was preparing me to help my mother journey through the pathway of healing. He was going to guard us and protect us, so my mother would have time to heal.

I walked over and said, "Mommy this has been an unforgettable tragedy for all of us. "Let"s pray mommy", I said. I know that God and the angels are watching over us and they are going to help us. We knelt down, prayed for the baby, and prayed for our family. After we prayed my mother looked at me and told me that she loved me and that she is very sad that she lost the baby, then she looked at me and said, "But you know I don"t need another child because I have you and you fill my life with eternal joy. "I love you, Stacey" "I love you too mom."

From that moment, my mother and I developed a special bond. Our relationship grew stronger and stayed like that, as the years progressed. When she needed a shoulder to lean on or someone just to listen, I was there for her. In addition, she did the same for me. I realized that our parents have the same needs that we do. From toddlers to adulthood we rely on our parents for everything. Whom do our parents go to when they need help or support? Now I know that I am that person. As I live on this earth, I will be their caretaker and when I fly to the heavens above I will do the same.

About The Author

I am married with three children. There is a whole world in front of us. This world has millions of opportunities just waiting for people such as myself to encounter. It does not matter what age you are. You can achieve anything you put your mind too.

MY ACCOMPLISHMENTS:

I graduated from Stockton College in Pomona, New Jersey. I am an H.O.P.E. Mentor, for the Epilepsy Foundation. I have spoken at different events for schools, organizations, political events, I spoke in front of Congress in Washington and anywhere my help is needed to educate people about epilepsy. I was on four talk shows. The interviews focused on the importance of understanding what epilepsy is, how to help someone having a seizure and giving people with epilepsy encouragement and hope for the future.

I have been on radio stations discussing epilepsy and I have appeared in many newspapers all over New Jersey such as, The Leader, Belleville Post and the Star Ledger. In addition, on June 26, 2002, I was honored an award by the Epilepsy Foundation of New Jersey for Outstanding Volunteer Award.

BOOKS WRITTEN BY STACEY CHILLEMI :

Epilepsy You're Not Alone

Epilepsy You're Not Alone is an inspirational self-help book that teaches people with epilepsy how to live a healthy and productive life. The book shares encouraging stories and gives readers a workable program for coping with their disorder enabling readers to overcome their disorder and get on with their lives.
http://www.iuniverse.com/bookstore/book_detail.asp?&isbn=0-595-19526-1

Eternal Love: Romantic Poetry Straight from the Heart

How can I find a person to love and share the rest of my life? Will true love come to me naturally? How can I build a relationship. The poems in my book answer these questions. People are eager to find true love—love that will not last a short period of time, but for a lifetime. Eternal Love is designed to answer these questions and more. It is divided into two sections that correspond with the way most people "experience" love: explanation of love (research) and the love poems (using poems and love letters that I created). Each part highlights a particular aspect of love, what love is, and how it can be obtained.
http://www.publishamerica.com/shopping/
shopdisplayproducts.asp?Search=Yes

My Mommy Has Epilepsy (Children's Book)

"My Mommy Has Epilepsy," helps educate children and help them understand what they can do if a friend or love one is having a seizure. There are so many myths that still roam through our society about epilepsy. gives children and their family truth; medical facts explained in simplistic terminology so there is a clear understanding about epilepsy.
http://www.lulu.com/content/93092

Keep the Faith: To Live and Be Heard from the Heavens Above (poetry book)

A person does not survive by bread alone. Life requires other things, and Faith and Love are amongst them. For many, perhaps for all, they are the only important things we have that keep us going each morning as we awake and each night as the sunsets. "Keep the Faith," brings inspiration to people's lives and a direction to follow.

http://www.lulu.com/content/117499

Live, Learn, and Be Happy with Epilepsy

"Live, Learn, and Be Happy with Epilepsy," will be a 200-page book targeted for individuals who have epilepsy. Unlike other books on epilepsy, it will focus on The History of Epilepsy, Learning How to Cope with Your Epilepsy, What is Epilepsy?, The Brain and Epilepsy, When Your Child Develops Epilepsy, Types of Seizures, Epilepsy Medications and Treatments, How to Boost Your Self-Esteem, Getting on with your Life, Learning How to Love Yourself Again, Say Goodbye to Stress and Hello to Happiness, Our Dreams Are Our Future, Let Your Confidence Be Your Strength, Worried, Lost, Confused?, How Keeping Yourself in Good Health Can Help Your Epilepsy, Glossary for epilepsy, and a Resource Guide to organizations, websites and other helpful resources.

http://www.lulu.com/content/124393

Epilepsy and Pregnancy: What Every Women Should Know

Co-authored by Dr. Blanca Vasques. Through my efforts, I have been able to show other women that it is not impossible to become a mother. I have given women and couples hope and a new look on life. Epilepsy is just a disorder. Your life does not end because you have epilepsy.

http://www.demosmedpub.com/
getpage.cfm?filename=book179.html&userid=64025494

I have received awards in my achievements and certificates in recognition for outstanding efforts in trying to improve society. I have been an active participant in organizations and activities. I have been a role model to many individuals.

I have written many articles on epilepsy, such as How Exercise Can Help Your Seizures, Coping with Epilepsy, Can Women with Epilepsy Have Babies and Why Children Have Seizures. She has also written self-help articles, such as 10 Steps to Self-confidence, Seven Steps to Loving Yourself, 4 Steps to High Self-esteem and Greatest relief for stress: Take some time each day for yourself.

I have appeared three times on News 12 on the talk show New Jersey Women and has had articles written about her efforts to help people with epilepsy. I have contributed time in helping people with epilepsy and making society more aware of the disorder. I have had epilepsy for 28 years.

My websites
http://inspirationallivingonline.com
http://www.authorsden.com/staceydchillemi

Printed in the United States
91608LV00005B/1/A

9 781413 775884